THE TEMPLE CHURCH

A HISTORY IN PICTURES

THE TEMPLE CHURCH

A HISTORY IN PICTURES

COMPILED BY

ROBIN GRIFFITH-JONES

MASTER OF

THE TEMPLE

This book originally accompanied an exhibition in the Church itself, in 2008. The book and exhibition were both linked with a conference, In Despight of the Devouring Flame: The History, Architecture and Effigies of the Temple Church, organised jointly by the Temple Church and the Courtauld Institute of Art and held at the Courtauld. It has been a pleasure and an education to work with David Park at the Courtauld.
The definitive work – which itself grew out of the 2008 conference – on the Church's architecture, monuments and decoration is now R. Griffith-Jones and D. Park (editors), The Temple Church (Woodbridge Boydell, 2010)

The book and exhibition were made possible by the generous help of many people, and we gladly acknowledge our great debt of gratitude to them all.

Those who sponsored or underwrote the exhibition:
Mr Tim Charlton QC and members of the Bar Golfing Society
The John S. Cohen Foundation
The Golden Bottle Trust
Professor Anthony Mellows, OBE, TD and Mrs Mellows
Mr Edward Nugee TD, QC

The lending institutions:
The Victoria and Albert Museum
The Bowes Museum, Barnard Castle

Those who gave us patient help:
Liz Clarke and Henrietta Amodio in the Church's office; Ian Garwood, Middle Temple's Director of Estates and a tireless friend to the Church; Clare Rider and Lesley Whitelaw, the archivists of Inner and Middle Temple, and their colleagues (Hannah Baker, Celia Charlton, Siobhan Woodgate and Frank Wright); John Fisher at the Guildhall Library; John Clark, Jackie Keily and John Schofield at the Museum of London; Jane Whittaker at the Bowes Museum; Paul Williamson and Victoria Jarvis at the Victoria & Albert Museum; Alan Borg and Pamela Willis at the Museum of the Order of St John.
Book designed by Maria Beddoes & Paul Khera.

We gratefully acknowledge the provision of photographs and permission to reproduce them from various sources, and our debt to various works of reference. They are listed in detail on p. 83.

For further history, details of current events and a virtual reality tour of the Church: www.templechurch.com.

This edition published by Pitkin Publishing 2011
ISBN 978 1 84165 359 4

THE TEMPLE CHURCH
A HISTORY IN PICTURES

Welcome to the Temple Church. You may be visiting it in person,
or just in the pages of this book. Either way, we hope that you
will enjoy the Church's beauty, its history and its numinous calm.
It has not always been so tranquil: the Knights Templar who built
it, eight hundred years ago, were bankers and diplomatic brokers
to successive kings; the Temple itself was at the centre of
England's religious, political and economic life.

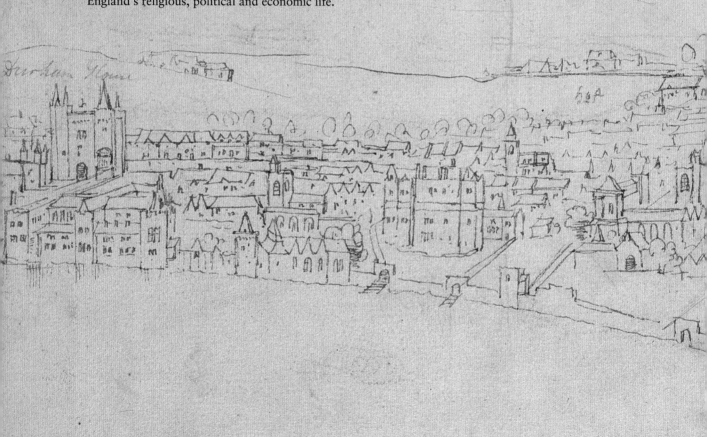

On the suppression of the Knights Templar the Church passed to the Knights Hospitaller. At the Reformation it reverted to the Crown, and in 1608 – when the Church was already over 400 years old – James I granted all the Templars' former land between Fleet Street and the River to the societies of Inner and Middle Temple, two of London's Inns of Court. (Every barrister in England and Wales must, to this day, still belong to one of the four Inns.) The Letters Patent commanded that the Inns 'shall serve for the accommodation and education of those studying and following the profession of the …laws, abiding in the same Inns, for all time to come.'

From Anthonis van den Wyngaerde, Panorama of London (1544). Collection: The Ashmolean Museum, Oxford. The Temple Church is on the right hand-edge of the facing page.

The Inns undertook in return that 'they will well and sufficiently maintain and keep up the aforesaid Church, the chancel and the belfry of the same...at their own expense, for the celebration there in perpetuity of divine service....' The Inns have done so, ever since, with a generosity that has re-beautified the Church in every generation.

This book was compiled to accompany an exhibition mounted in the Round Church in 2008 as part of the Festival with which the two Inns of Court celebrated the 400th Anniversary of the King's grant. All of us in the Church are proud to serve the Inns as our predecessors have served them for four centuries.

The Church is, above all else, an active, living Church within the Church of England. Whether you work in the City, live in London or are among our many visitors from around the world, you are most welcome to rejoin us for our services at which we acknowledge the loving Creator of us all, in whose sight a thousand ages are like an evening gone.

Jerusalem:
The Centre of the World

Mappa Mundi (in Hereford Cathedral), made c. 1295 under the patronage or direction of 'Richard of Holdingham and Sleaford', probably Richard de Bello, prebendary in Lincoln, 1276-83, is the largest and most beautiful of the medieval maps of the world (1625 x 1370 mm). Richard's inscription asks for the prayers of all who shall hear, see or read the map's 'estoire' or 'history'. The map tells the story of the world.

Jerusalem is the circular city at the map's centre. *This is Jerusalem, says the Lord: I have set her in the midst of the nations round about her* (Ezekiel 5.5). The map has the east at its top. Here, on the top rim, is the Garden of Eden. Asia occupies the top half of the map; Europe the bottom left; Africa the bottom right. The Mediterranean stretches down from Jerusalem to the Pillars of Hercules at the bottom rim. In Italy, on its left, is Rome, 'that holds the reins of the round world.' Great Britain and Ireland, on the north-western limits of the world, are the islands in the lower left corner. Scotland is divided from England by the Tweed, Wales by the Dee and Severn.

Above the earth sits Christ in majesty. His angels sound the trumpets that announce the Last Judgement. Looped to the circle around the world itself are four rings, each with one gold letter. Together they spell out the word MORS, death. At the map's bottom right-hand corner a horseman waves back to the map from which he has learnt. He is leaving it now and heading out into the world. A huntsman with a brace of greyhounds bids the horseman farewell: 'Passe avant', 'Go forward'.

We are now used to maps with the north at the top. The Mappa Mundi is most easily read if the page is turned 90 degrees clockwise.

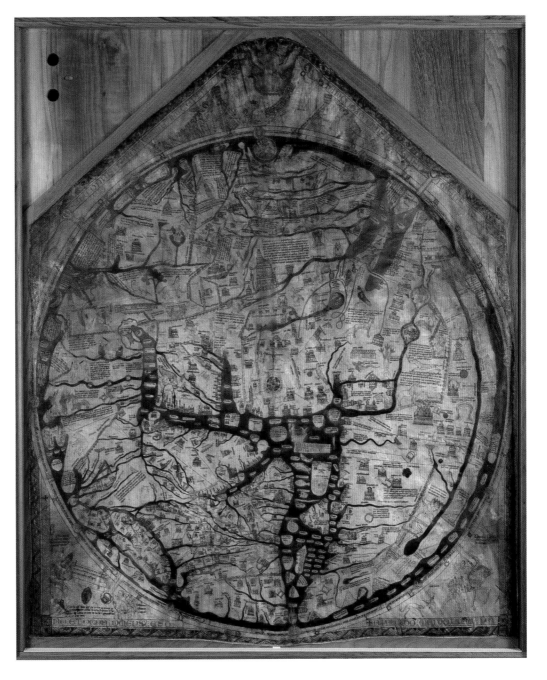

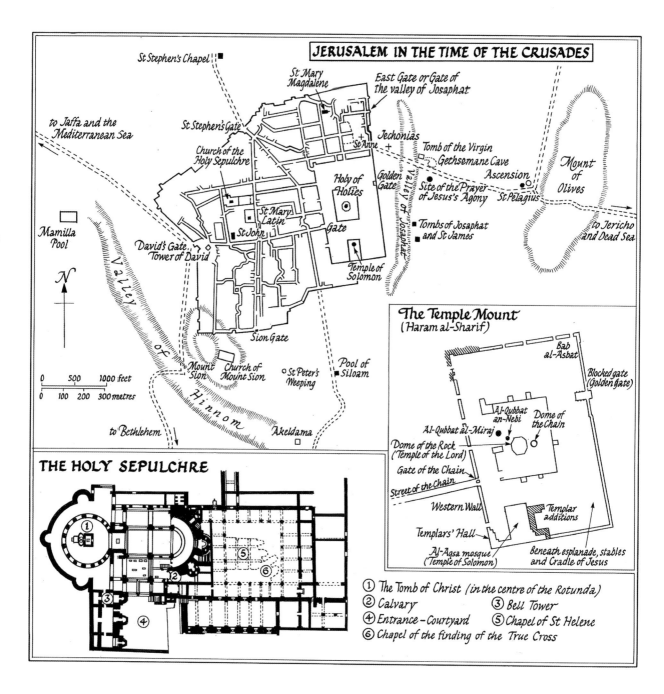

JERUSALEM IN THE TIME OF THE CRUSADES

St Stephen's Chapel

St Mary Magdalene

East Gate or Gate of the valley of Josaphat

to Jaffa and the Mediterranean Sea

St Stephen's Gate

Jechonias

St Anne

Tomb of the Virgin

Church of the Holy Sepulchre

Gethsemane Cave

Ascension

Mount of Olives

Holy of Holies

Golden Gate

Site of the Prayer of Jesus's Agony

St Pelagius

St Mary Latin

Gate

Valley of Josaphat

to Jericho and Dead Sea

St John

Tombs of Josaphat and St James

12

Mamilla Pool

David's Gate. Tower of David

Temple of Solomon

N

Valley

Sion Gate

of

Hinnom

Mount Sion

Church of Mount Sion

St Peter's Weeping

Pool of Siloam

0   500   1000 feet
0   100   200   300 metres

to Bethlehem

Akeldama

The Temple Mount
(Haram al-Sharif)

Bab al-Asbat

Blocked gate (Golden gate)

Al-Qubbat an-Nebi

Dome of the Chain

Al-Qubbat al-Miraj

Dome of the Rock (Temple of the Lord)

Gate of the Chain

Street of the chain

Western Wall

Templar additions

Templars' Hall

Al-Aqsa mosque (Temple of Solomon)

Beneath esplanade, stables and Cradle of Jesus

THE HOLY SEPULCHRE

① The Tomb of Christ (in the centre of the Rotunda)
② Calvary   ③ Bell Tower
④ Entrance – Courtyard   ⑤ Chapel of St Helene
⑥ Chapel of the finding of the True Cross

THE HOLY SEPULCHRE

The most sacred place in the most sacred city of Jerusalem was the site of Jesus' own death, burial and rising: the Church of the Holy Sepulchre. It was the goal of every pilgrim. Christ's (supposed) cave-tomb had been rediscovered in 325; the Emperor Constantine built over the cave a shrine, a courtyard and basilica to the east, and finally a colossal round church encircling the shrine itself. In every round church that the Templars built throughout Europe they recreated the sanctity of this holy place. To walk into our Round Church was to walk into Jerusalem.

'To the tomb of Christ!' So Pope Urban II, preaching the First Crusade in 1095, called upon the people of Europe. The language of the crusades was the language of feudal loyalty: the love of vassals for their liege-lord Christ who had been robbed of his patrimony and called for his honour to be satisfied.

The Order of 'the poor fellow-soldiers of Jesus Christ' was founded in 1118-9; its knights took vows of poverty, chastity and obedience, and dedicated themselves to the protection of pilgrims. The Latin King of Jerusalem gave them space for accommodation near his own palace on the Temple Mount, site of the long-destroyed Jewish Temple; so the Order was soon known as the Knights Templar. At their foundation the Templars were deeply suspect: it was unnatural for one man to be soldier and monk together. But they won the support of the most powerful monk of the age, Bernard of Clairvaux.

Bernard wrote *In Praise of the New Knighthood* for and about the order and those it served. He wrote of Jerusalem and above all of the Holy Sepulchre itself. There a knight should be raised up to thoughts of Christ's death and of the freedom from death that it had won for Christ's people: 'The death of Christ is the death of my death.' Bernard draws on Paul's famous account of baptism: '*For we are buried with him by baptism into death: that like as Christ was raised up from the dead by the glory of the Father, even so we should walk in newness of life* (Romans 6.4-5). How sweet it is for pilgrims after the great weariness of a long journey, after so many dangers of land and sea, there to rest at last where they know their Lord has rested!'

The Templars in London: 12th and early 13th Centuries

The Templars had their first London base in Holborn a mile to the north of the present Temple, and there they built a round church. Their property became known as 'the Temple'. By the 1160s, however; they were on the move: they sold their Holborn site to the Bishop of Lincoln in 1161, and moved to the present 'New' Temple by the river.

At the time of the Templars' arrival, London was acquiring the status of the kingdom's capital. The kings' removal of the centre of government from Winchester to Westminster recognised the already established commercial importance of London, and led to Westminster's development as both the spiritual and the bureaucratic centre of the realm. No wonder the Templars chose for their new house a site alongside the street which linked the two poles of the new capital: to the east, the city around St Paul's; and to the west, Westminster around the King.

In 1162 or soon after, Thomas Becket granted an indulgence of twenty days to all those who entered the Church, especially on the anniversary of its founding. In 1163 Geoffrey de Mandeville was buried here, in the cemetery or 'the porch before the west door of the Church'. This site – with a church and cemetery, both consecrated – was already the Templars' London home. Early in 1185 Heraclius, Latin Patriarch of Jerusalem, was in London to seek support – and perhaps a king – for the Kingdom of Jerusalem. On 10 February he consecrated the Church in honour of the Blessed Virgin Mary.

Immediately to the south of the Round, the lower floor of St Anne's Chapel, with two vaults and access from the Round, may have been built in these early years. The upper floor, with three vaults, is likely to have been added in a different campaign, probably when the present Chancel was built (1235-40). Remains of the lower storey were uncovered in the 1860s and again in the 1940s.

The Temple Church

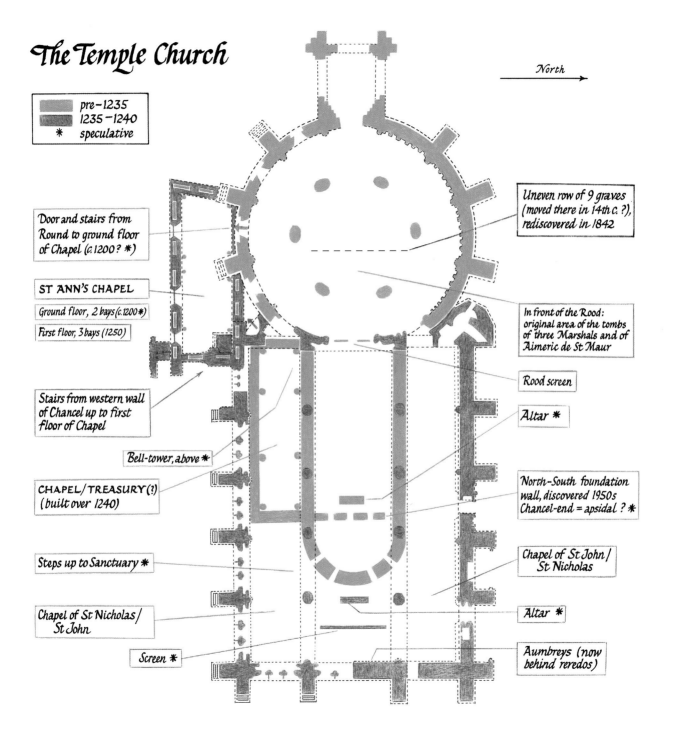

North →

Legend:
- pre–1235
- 1235–1240
- * speculative

Door and stairs from Round to ground floor of Chapel (c. 1200? *)

ST ANN'S CHAPEL
Ground floor, 2 bays (c. 1200 *)
First floor, 3 bays (1250)

Stairs from western wall of Chancel up to first floor of Chapel

Bell-tower, above *

CHAPEL/TREASURY (?) (built over 1240)

Steps up to Sanctuary *

Chapel of St Nicholas / St John

Screen *

Uneven row of 9 graves (moved there in 14th c.?), rediscovered in 1842

In front of the Rood: original area of the tombs of three Marshals and of Aimeric de St Maur

Rood screen

Altar *

North-South foundation wall, discovered 1950s Chancel-end = apsidal? *

Chapel of St John / St Nicholas

Altar *

Aumbreys (now behind reredos)

The buildings raised against the wall were in the 1860s at last removed (see above). There were ample traces of medieval plaster on the undressed Kentish stone. The buttresses' front faces were found to curve in sympathy with the curve of the Round's wall; the buttresses are oddly disparate, revealing the Church's piecemeal repair over time. The capitals of the nook-shafts (flanking the windows) can be seen; their columns were to be reinstated in the 1860s. The build-up of earth, accumulated over centuries and hiding the wall's lower courses, had just been removed and the tombs revealed.

What was the shape of the drum's original roof? Wyngaerde in 1544 shows a cone (p. 6). A report of 1653 mentions 'the steeple'. Emmett's stylised print of the 1680s (p. 46) shows a shallow dome; and according to an account of 1720, 'You enter first into a large Circular Tower, which on the top terminates in something like a dome.' The roof inspected in 1840, and clearly of some antiquity, was a shallow timber cone, in wood.

18

THE WEST DOOR

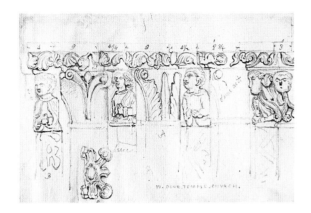

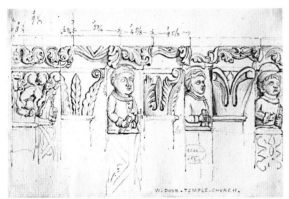

This doorway, though badly weathered and often repaired, remains majestic. How much of the elaborately carved stonework is 12th century? The jambs (flanking the door itself) are 19th century; so is the innermost order of the rounded arch; so, as we know from a report of 1838, are the columns. The surrounding porch is late 19th century.

Four busts surmount the columns on each side. Each quartet is carved from just two stones. The four figures on the north side are wearing caps or turbans, those on the south are bare-headed; all are beardless. Several are wearing a tight-fitting garment with buttons down the front. Can the figures be identified? The tight-fitting, buttoned clothes may be significant: before the 14th century, buttons were thought of as oriental; some of the door's figures may, then, represent the Moslems whom the Templars were called to fight.

F. Nash, c. 1818: Drawings of the Busts on the West Doorway. Collection: The Society of Antiquaries of London.

Facing page: F.Nash, c. 1818: The West Doorway.

A chapel to the south of the original Chancel, its floor 2 metres lower than the Chancel floor, was discovered after World War II. The southern aisle of the new, broader Chancel was built over it, 1235-40; the chapel's vaulting was destroyed and all access to it was abandoned. (The masons building the new Chancel used the plastered walls as a drawing-board, setting out the curves of their new vaults.) Little survives of the chapel except this column and beautiful capital at its west end, some traces of wall-decoration, and at its east end two lockers and a double piscina. There were once three windows in the south wall; the ground-level must have fallen away sharply towards the river. These windows were blocked up while the chapel was still in use; the chapel has been tentatively identified as the Temple's treasury.

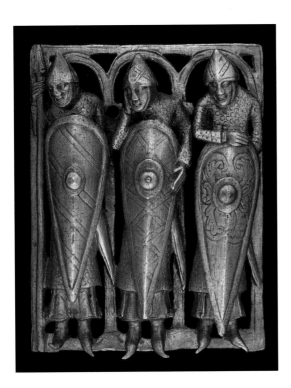

'The Temple Pyx', c. 1150. This copper-alloy plaque (92 x 72 mm) was said in 1833 to have been found in the Temple Church 'during some of the repairs which have of late taken place in that edifice.' The knights' similarity to our effigies might have given rise to the story; there is evidence of a quite different provenance. The plaque may have been made as part of a Holy Sepulchre group, showing the guards asleep at Jesus' tomb; the resurrection would then have been visible through the pierced arches.
Collection: The Burrell Collection, Glasgow.

A 14th century pilgrim-badge (discovered in Tudor Street) showing the flagellation of Henry II at Canterbury in penance for the murder of Thomas Becket at Canterbury. Thomas Becket called himself 'Thomas of London' throughout his life. After his martyrdom in 1170 the City of London put itself under his patronage; he joined St Paul on the Mayor's and the Corporation's seals. Becket was particularly revered by English crusaders; the Order of Thomas of Acon (Acre) was founded in his honour. There was a chapel to Thomas across the courtyard to the south of the Temple Church; the inventory of the Church's goods in 1308 included 'one sword with which the blessed Thomas of Canterbury was killed.'
Collection: The Museum of London.

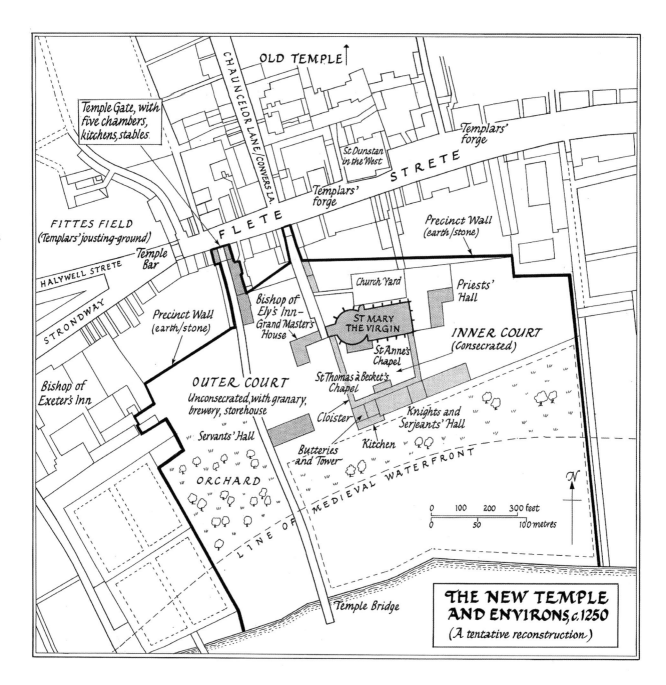

22

THE NEW TEMPLE
AND ENVIRONS, c. 1250
(A tentative reconstruction)

The Chancel

In 1235 Henry III bequeathed his body by charter 'to the Blessed Mary and the House of the Chivalry of the Temple, London;' his Queen made the same bequest of her own body. In 1237 the King – no doubt with his future burial in mind – endowed, by a perpetual payment of £8 per annum to the Master and Brethren of the Temple, three chaplains to celebrate daily three masses there, 'one for us, one for all Christian people, and one for the faithful departed.' It was surely with a view to these burials that the Templars demolished their single-bay chancel and built in its place the Church's present 'Hall Church': a chancel of three bays of equal height, ensuring a flood of light to the full height of the central aisle.

Here is a tentative sketch of the New Temple in the years after the Church's long three-bay chancel was dedicated on Ascension Day 1240 in the presence of the king. The area conformed to the familiar layout of a large monastery: an outer, unconsecrated courtyard; and an inner, consecrated courtyard with the Church, cemetery and accommodation for monks and priests.

In the restoration of the 1840s, remains were found of coloured decoration on the Chancel's vaulted ceiling: 'colours and metallic plating in straight-sided oblongs, with semi-circular heads.' Some medieval stonework had at some time been re-used to block up the openings on the triforium in the Round. These were reopened in the 1840s, and further decoration was discovered on the old stones: bands of rich colour (yellow, red and blue) on a yellow or chalk ground, and some more metallic plating.

These aumbries (in which to keep the vessels used at Mass) are now hidden behind the Wrenian reredos at the Chancel's east end. Their shape in the early 20th century (as above) was probably due to early 17th century restoration; the central opening may have been created for a mural decoration. In 1929 the aumbries were restored to an earlier disposition: four equal and deeper openings with trefoil tops. Small rebates at the front and bolt holes suggest that they were once fronted with doors.

St Anne's Chapel to the south of the Round, damaged in a fire in 1678, was finally demolished in 1826. In this watercolour (p. 27), the surrounding houses have already been taken down. In the chapel's upper storey is the springing for a three-bay vault. The door to the staircase down to the Chancel is in the furthest bay. On the left-hand edge, a classical door-frame adorns a 12th century entrance; inside the Round, this doorway had been surmounted by an inscription (since destroyed, and now copied over the main West Door) marking the Round's dedication in 1185.

Above: 'Penitential cell', whose two narrow windows can be seen in the north-west corner of the Chancel. When Walter Bacheler, Preceptor of Ireland, was charged with theft of the Order's property, he was kept imprisoned in chains for eight weeks and died; he may have been refused burial in consecrated land. In the 19th century this small room was identified as his cell.

Below: Tile from the Chancel, 1240 or later, of a style and manufacture ("Westminster tiles") familiar at the time. Collection: The Museum of London.

Facing page: Copy of a watercolour by J. Buckler, 1826: St Anne's Chapel.

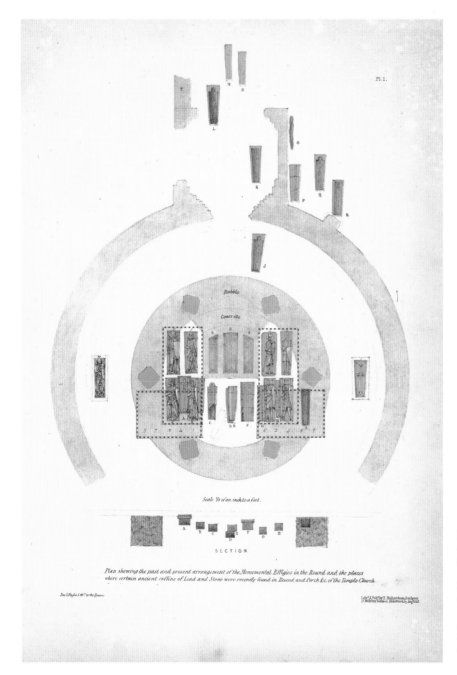

Left: E. Richardson, 1845: Effigies and (beneath floor-level) coffins in the round.

Facing page: The five effigies laid out on the north side of the Round, 1682-1841. From R. Gough, Sepulchral Monuments…(1786). Collection: The Society of Antiquaries of London.

The Effigies in the Round

In 1841 Edward Richardson, in his repairs to the Round, made a record of the lead and stone coffins he found under its floor; here (p. 28) is his own plan of the discoveries. He has superimposed three levels of information.

- Most prominently he shows the new arrangement of the effigies for which he himself was responsible, 1841-45, and which survives today: two groups of four, laid out in pairs on either side of the Round's central area (and outlined here in red); and one outrider on each side, an effigy on the left (south) side and a coped stone on the right (north) side. He has numbered the figures and the stone 1-10. (The southern outrider had been brought into the Church c.1682.)

- Richardson has also shown, in the lower (eastern) part of the Round's centre, two rectangles bearing, out of order, the numbers 1-10. This records the layout of the ten memorials – nine effigies and the coped stone – from 1682 until 1841 (outlined here in green). There are two lines of five memorials each; the numbers relate that old layout, seen above in Gough's print of 1786, to Richardson's.

- Richardson has also indicated in his plan where he had found lead and stone coffins under the floor. Most intriguing is the untidy row of nine coffins just below (to the east of) the centre. They are marked by Richardson with the capital letters A-I. At the bottom of the plan Richardson has added a sectional view of this row.

It is not clear when the row of coffins was laid out nor how it ever related to the eight principal effigies. But we are likely to look for a clue in an account of the mid-17th century: 'Within a spacious grate of Iron, in the midst of the round walk, under the Steeple, do ly eight Statues in Military Habits; each of them having large and deep Shields on their left Armes. Of which five are cross legged. There are also three other Gravestones lying about five inches above the level ground; on one which is a large Escocheon with a Lion rampant graven thereon.' Such a single row of effigies would of course have obstructed any processional use of the Round's main west-east axis.

E. Richardson, 1845: A Lead Tomb from the Round.

Richardson gave a full description of this effigy. The knight had long been identified, no doubt in part because of the lion rampant (a Marshal emblem) on his shield, as William Marshal, 1st Earl of Pembroke. Richardson canonised an alternative ascription: this knight, he claimed, was the 2nd Earl. Richardson, in reorganising the effigies, put together on the south side the three knights which he identified as Earls of Pembroke; he saw the older man, now the south-western member of the group, as the great 1st Earl.

Richardson removed layers of later paint from the present figure and described what he discovered beneath. 'Traces of delicate flesh colour remained on the face. The embattled tower had some red left on it; the mouldings some light green… Traces of gilding appeared on the ring-mail throughout…The buckles, spurs and squirrel [supporting the shield] had also been gilt. There were some traces of the surcoat which had upon it considerable remains of crimson lake; the underside, of light blue…'

Given the effigies' relocation over time, can we tell where they originally stood and which effigy represents which of the knights known to have been buried here? William Marshal, 1st Earl of Pembroke (d. 1219) became one of the most famous knights of his age when he unhorsed the young Richard Coeur de Lion and won his favour; William would be a crucial mediator between King John and the barons, and Regent for the child King Henry III. William was buried here 'before the high cross', that is, in front of the rood screen dividing the Round Church from the Chancel. His eldest son William (d. 1231), an executor to Magna Carta, was buried 'near his father', and his third son Gilbert (d. 1241) 'near to his father and brother'. Aymeric de St Maur, Master of the Knights Templar in England, had asked to be buried beside the 1st Earl.

It is hard to be sure now how the effigies once looked in detail. Richardson restored and partly recut them; in 1941 the Round's burning roof fell in on them. Crossed legs were a convention, familiar from manuscripts and stained glass, to show animation: such figures were imagined as walking towards the viewer. Most of the effigies showed their knights in their early thirties, the prime of life at which Christ died and at which the dead will rise on his return.

The effigy identified since 1841 as the effigy of William Marshal, 1st Earl of Pembroke: in 1786; in the late 19th century; after the bomb-damage of 10 May 1941; and today.

34

Below: The Tomb of a Bishop, 13th century, formerly lying over its coffin near the south-east corner of the Chancel, now in a 19th century niche nearby. This is the best preserved of the Church's effigies. When the tomb was opened in 1810 the skeleton, a crozier and fragments of the robes were found in good preservation. A child's skeleton lay at the bishop's feet; William Plantagenet, fifth son of Henry III, who died as an infant in 1256, is said to have been buried in the Church.

Right: The marks of medieval stone-masons, found on stonework in the restoration of the 1860s.

THE END OF THE ORDER

On Friday 13 October 1307 every Templar house in the Kingdom of France was occupied by the bailiffs of King Philip the Fair; the knights were arrested, put into solitary confinement, and notified that the King knew of the wickedness to which the Order had succumbed; in particular, that at their secret rites of initiation knights must deny Christ, spit or urinate on the cross and submit to sodomitic ritual. The knights' options were made clear: those who confessed would have a penance imposed and then be reconciled to the Church; those who protested their innocence would be tortured. It is not surprising that the King of France secured, for the most part, the confessions he sought.

King Philip had reasons enough to attack this famously wealthy Order: he was in deep debt and desperately short of gold with which to revalue his coinage; he had already taken what he could from the Jews and the Lombards, the other groups dominant in his Kingdom's finance; and the Templars – who had lost their last toe-hold in the Holy Land in 1291 and with it the rationale for their existence – were badly governed, unaccountable and unpopular. The Templars were a natural target; and if the King's agents were indeed able to persuade him of the Order's guilt, the pious (by our standards, superstitious) King would have been determined to rid his realm of a corruption so likely to bring down the wrath of God.

Were any of the Templars guilty of any of the crimes alleged? Most (not quite all) modern scholars believe that the charges were trumped up by King Philip and his agents. The other kings of Europe acted slowly and reluctantly against the Order; in England Edward II resisted the use of torture for two years and dispersed the knights to other monasteries.

Facing page: A 14th century corbel from the Temple Church. Collection: The Museum of London

Sir Edmund Plowden (d. 1584), Treasurer of Middle Temple 1561-6 and largely responsible for the building of its Hall (still one of the most beautiful buildings in London, 500 yards south-west of the Church); author of highly influential Commentaries on law; a Roman Catholic at a time when Roman Catholics were under deep suspicion, and buried at his own request in the (Anglican) Temple Church, the church of the Inn he had served so well. His epitaph: 'I have lived in a dangerous channel; I die in harbour.'

Richard Martin (d. 1608) was 'a very handsome man, a graceful speaker, facetious and well-loved,' arranged riotous parties in Middle Temple, and took fifteen years to qualify as a barrister. Despite this wild youth, he became Recorder of London.

Richard Hooker
at the Temple

Richard Hooker was appointed Master of the Temple in 1585. England
was in alarm. The threat from Catholic Europe had revived: there had been
rebellion against the Queen and Settlement in 1569; the Pope in 1570 had
excommunicated Elizabeth and declared her subjects free from their
allegiance; Mary Queen of Scots was linked with ever further conspiracy
against her cousin; and the danger of Spanish invasion was growing.
England's radical reformers looked to the example of Calvin's godly state,
Geneva. The 'head and neck' of English Calvinism were Thomas
Cartwright and Walter Travers. Since 1581 Travers had been the Reader of
the Temple. Roman Catholic recusants were known to be sheltered there,
most famously Sir Edmund Plowden.

When Hooker carefully and bravely explored the possibility that individual
Roman Catholics could be saved, the scene was set for the most famous
public debate of the day. Hooker was as certain as Travers that Rome was in
error. But Rome's doctrines were built on the 'foundation of faith': salvation
through faith in Christ. A living and salvific faith, Hooker maintained, was
therefore possible for Roman Catholics. And Rome's supposed errors? Hooker
distinguished between the responsibility that Rome's teachers bore
for their heresy and the error into which it led their unwitting people.
Hooker's concern was acutely pastoral: to reassure those who feared for
their forebears' salvation. 'I must confess unto you,' said Hooker: 'if it be
an error to think that God may be merciful to save men, even when they
err, my greatest comfort is my error. Were it not for the love I bear unto this
"error", I would neither wish to speak nor to live.'

The debate led Hooker to an ever deeper exploration of the disputes between
the different churches which became his masterpiece, a foundational document
of Anglican theology: The Laws of Ecclesiastical Polity.

The Letters Patent, 1608

In 1608 King James I granted the Temple to the two Inns of Court, Inner and Middle Temple. He stipulated that the Inns 'shall serve for the accommodation and education of those studying and following the profession of the ...laws, abiding in the same Inns, for all time to come.' The Inns have remained, ever since, central to the legal and ethical formation of the barristers of England and Wales. The Inns must maintain the Church and its clergyman, the Master of the Temple. They must provide the Master with a mansion (which they do) and with a stipend of £17 6s 8d or 52 marks per annum (which, with a welcome allowance for four centuries' inflation, they do too).

Facing page: Thomas Greene, Treasurer of Middle Temple 1630, commissioned a book illustrating the heraldic glass in Middle Temple Hall. For its frontispiece he had this watercolour made of a Templar, duly adorned on his chest with a Lamb and Flag, an emblem of the Templars adopted by Middle Temple as its own.

This page: For the safe-keeping of the Inns' Letters Patent from James I, an ironbound chest with two locks was made (at the cost of £7 12s 4d to each Inn) and was kept under the communion table in the Church. By 1865 each Inn had the key to one of the chest's two padlocks.

42

Left: Two of four silver-gilt flagons, 1637, 343mm high, formerly used in the Church; two of the four belong to Inner and two to Middle Temple. (Maker's mark: RM in shield.)

Right: Two silver-gilt chalices, 1609, 245mm high, commissioned by the Inns for the Church's use in acknowledgement of the Letters Patent. From the Inner Temple Account Book, 1609-10: 'To Terry, a goldsmith, for two new communion cups for the Temple church, abating of the exchange of one old one, £13 12s 2d; the Middle Temple paid the one half, £6 16s 1d.' (Maker's mark: FT in monogram.)

Facing page: J. Ogilby, Map of the Temple (1677), showing in red the western limit of the Great Fire of London (1666) and – in newly imposed green – the approximate extent of the fire in winter 1678. (With temperatures well below freezing in 1678, there was insufficient water with which to combat the fire. Some younger members of Inner Temple fought the flames with beer instead; it was six years before Inner Temple settled the brewer's bill.)

Overleaf: The Temple in 1671 (print re-issued in 1770).

43

Plan of the Inner & Middle Temple copied by order of John Locke, Esq., Q.C., M.P., Treasurer, 1871. From the Map of London, 1677, by John Ogilby.

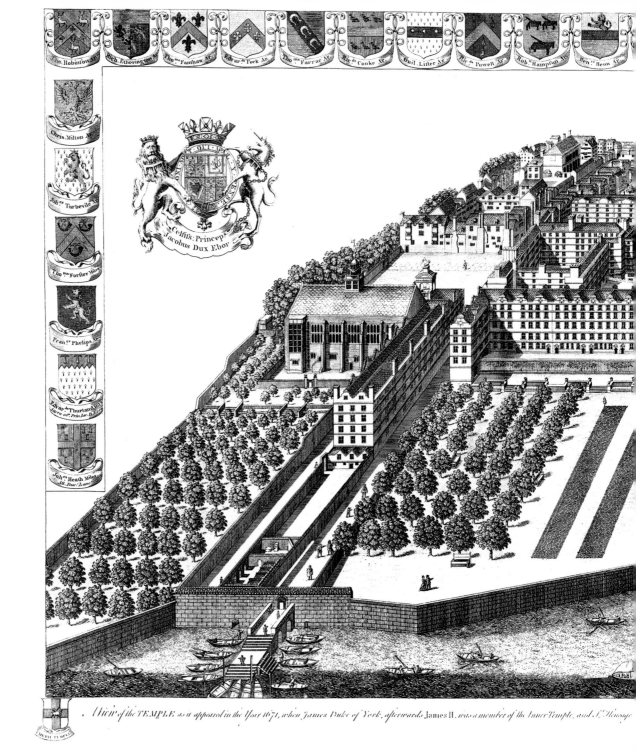

Tho. Robinson Ar. Reb. Etherington Ar. Tho's. Fanshaw Ar. Edvard Peck Ar. Tho'ma Farrar Ar. Ric'd. Cooke Ar. Guil. Lifter Ar. Ric'd. Powell Ar. Rob't. Hampfon Ar. Benj'n. Henn Ar.

Chris. Milton Ar.

Joh'es. Turbevile Ar.

Tho'ma. Forfter Miles

Fran'es. Phelips Ar.

Edvard Thurland Miles
(turn of) Prin. Inr. B. 1674

Joh'es. Heath Miles
(H. Duc. Lanc.)

Celfts: Princeps
Jacobus Dux Ebor

View of the TEMPLE as it appeared in the Year 1671, when James Duke of York, afterwards James II. was a member of the Inner Temple, and S'r. Heneage

...ight & Bar.t Attorn Gen.l afterwards L.d Keeper, L.d Chancellor & Earl of Nottingham, was Treasurer of that Honorable Society, at whose expence the same is now re-engraved An.o 1770.

THE SOUTH SIDE OF THE TEMPLE CHURCH

W.ᵐ Emmett Fecit

Two stylised views of the Church, 1702, by William Emmett, who also carved some of
the Church's woodwork under Christopher Wren. On the inside, open screens divide the
Round Church from the Chancel; the Round's windows are given pointed (gothic) tops.
On the outside (shown without St Anne's Chapel or the further buildings on the south side),
flaming acorns adorn the three gables at the east end and the buttresses to the Round have
been given a classical profile. Most striking are the shallow domes shown (or imagined) on
the porch (which was in fact surmounted by a building) and the Round.

Collection (p. 47): Guildhall Library, City of London.

To y̱ᵉ Worshipfuil y̱ᵉ Treasurer y̱ᵉ Maʳˢ.
of y̱ᵉ Bench and y̱ᵉ rest of y̱ᵉ Membʳˢ.
of y̱ᵉ Honᵇˡᵉˢ Society of y̱ᵉ Middle and
Inner Temple. Humble Dedicated by
your Servant Wᴹ Emmett

The Classical Refurbishment

Christopher Wren (whose first marriage was solemnised in the Temple Church in 1669) was asked for advice after the fire of 1678, and was commissioned to refurbish the Church in classical style. These and the following pages show the results. The joinery cost £570 2s 6d, of which £45 was paid to 'William Emmett, Carver, for carving work about the altarpiece, pillar, pilasters, shields, festoons, etc.' Almost all the Wrenian woodwork was sold in the refurbishments of the 1840s; the altarpiece and two columns were acquired by the Bowes Museum (Barnard Castle). After World War II the altarpiece was bought back for the Church; it still bore the number, 'Lot 24' from the 19th century sale. Of the two column-capitals, one was carved by Emmett, the other – of lower quality – by Thomas Lowe. The pulpit went to Christ Church, Greyfriars and was destroyed in the War.

The inventory of the Temple Church's contents, 1308, had included 'two pairs of organs' (ie, two ranks of pipes) and, in the vestry, 'twenty-two banners, eleven chasubles or mass vestments of divers colours, twenty-eight choir copes and four little copes for the choristers.' Since the 17th century the Temple Church has again been a centre of London's music.

The clerk to the Church in the 1660s, John Playford, was the first publisher of Henry Purcell's music and had a bookshop in the porch outside the west door. For five years, 1682-7, the Inns discussed the installation of a new organ. Two organ-makers were in contention: Father Smith and Renatus Harris. (The competition became intense. Each builder was loaned £100 by his sponsoring Inn to mount a guard, 24 hours a day, against sabotage.) The 'Battle of the Organs' was finally resolved by Judge Jeffreys of Inner Temple, who judiciously decided in favour of Smith, the candidate favoured by Middle. The result was one of the finest organs in London, installed in the central arch between Round and Chancel over a screen which extended across the full width of the Church.

When the blind John Stanley was organist of the Inner Temple (1734-86), it was not uncommon to see forty or fifty other organists, including Handel, gathered in the Church to hear him play.

The TEMPLE ORGAN, in its original position, on the SCREEN.

Facing page, Above: The shop in the West Porch, perhaps late 17th century. Published in The Gentleman's Magazine 54, Dec. 1784, opp. p. 911.

Facing page, Below: R.W. Billings, 1838: View from the north-east corner of the Chancel, with the box-pews, the central pulpit, and the organ and its screen across the west end of the Chancel.

The South East Prospect of the Temple Church

B. Cole, South-east Prospect of the Temple Church. Behind the buildings on the left is St Anne's Chapel. The area on the ground marked in dark green and grey was occupied by Lamb Building, destroyed in 1941; the present Church Court has existed only since the War.

Facing page: T. Malton, 1792: South-west View of the Round. The upper drum of the Round is battlemented. The windows have stone frames (and no nook-shafts). The classical doorway from the Round is visible to the left of the shops.

Left: T. Rowlandson and A.C. Pugin, 1809: Interior of the Round Church from the North-East. Monuments adorn the walls and columns; the columns are cased in wood. The round window over the main door is blocked. In the second bay to its left is the classical doorway seen from the other side in Malton's view of the exterior (p. 53); and in the next bay, the arch of the medieval doorway down to the lower floor of St Anne's Chapel. The sequence of carved heads is interrupted by the classical doorway and by the monument to the right of the main door; the windows in at least two bays appear to be blocked (to accommodate the buildings raised against the outer wall). The effigies are laid out in two rows of five: their disposition, 1682-1841.

Right: T. Malton, 1796: Interior of the Round Church from the South-East.

Facing page: J. Coney, 1805: Interior of the Round Church. The Round is isolated from the Chancel by the organ and screens.

By the early 19th century taste had changed. In 1808 the Church's decoration was described as an 'odious Wrenian overlay of doorways, windows, entablatures and scroll-shores.' By 1819 the Inns began to clear away the buildings nestling up against the Church's walls; in 1826 the Chapel of St Anne was finally demolished. Over the coming years the Church was restored under the direction of Robert Smirke, inside and out: the battlements were removed from the Round and the Chancel's south lancets repaired.

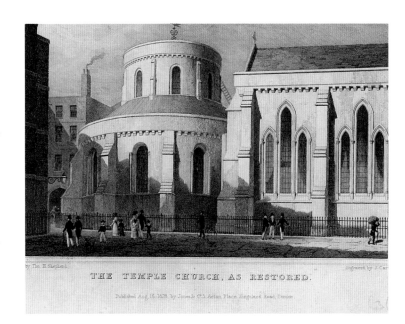

Facing page: G. Shepherd, 1811: Interior of the Chancel. Collection: Guildhall Library, City of London.

Above: W. Pearson, c. 1810: The Temple Church from the North. Collection: Guildhall Library, City of London.

Below: T.H. Shepherd, c. 1828: The Round Church, with the battlements removed, the buttresses reshaped and the Round's window-surrounds reconfigured.

THE TEMPLE CHURCH, AS RESTORED.

Published Aug. 15, 1828, by Jones & C°. Acton Place, Kingsland Road, London.

In the 1820s the arcading in the Round was renewed and the ancient heads in Caen stone were replaced by newly carved heads – some of them copies – in Portland stone. (Six on the north side, hidden behind monuments, were not replaced until the 1840s.) There was indignation, when some of the old heads were found to be in use as cart-wheel crutches; there has been sorrow at the heads' loss, ever since.

J.T. Smith, 1811: The Arcading in the Round Church before the Renewal of the Heads. The man with the chewed ear was among those copied in the renewal (p. 59, upper left).

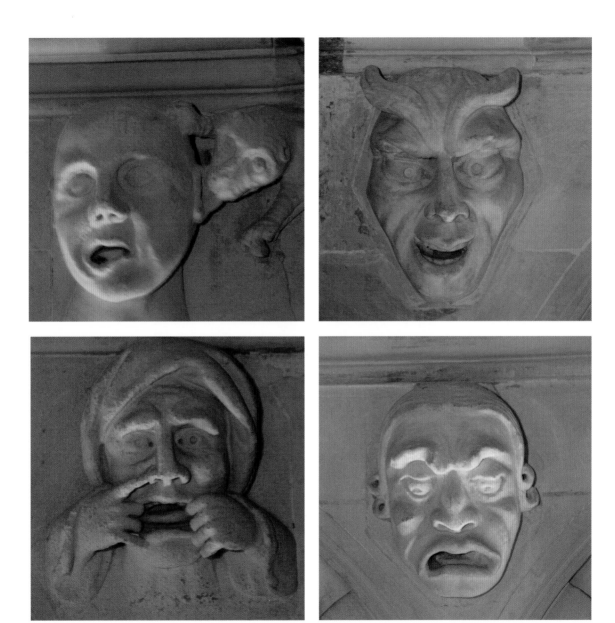

60

R.H. Essex, 1843: The Chancel;
and (facing page) Elevation of
the Altar Piece, to the designs of
S. Smirke and D. Burton.

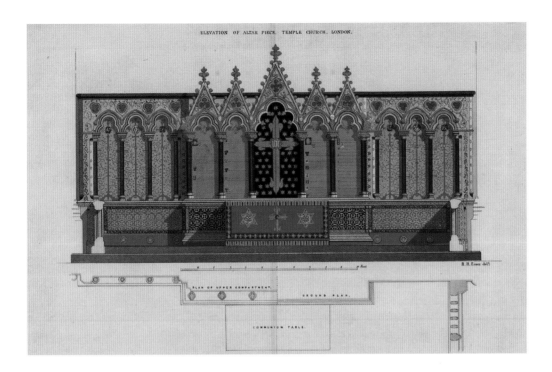

THE 1840's

In the 1840s the whole Church was restored and decorated in the grandest gothic style, under the direction initially of James Savage and then, when costs had overrun drastically, of Sidney Smirke (Robert's youngest brother) and Decimus Burton. The 17th century woodwork was disposed of in a series of sales. Here is an advertisement for just one of them:

To Architects, Church Building Committees, &c. – Removed from the Temple Church. – Magnificent carved Oak Pulpit, reading and Clerks' Desks, antique Columns, Capitals, Plaster Gothic Casts, Models, and Enrichments, and various Fittings, &c. MR. HAMMOND will SELL by AUCTION, for the Honourable Societies of the Inner and Middle Temples, at his spacious Rooms, 28 Chancery-lane, on Thursday, Nov. 10, at 12 for 1, the matchless and elegant PULPIT, with reading and clerks' desks, and staircase, profusely decorated with exquisite oak carvings after Grimlin Gibbons (sic), quantity of church seats, and the choice and valuable collection of models and enrichments in the Gothic style, used in the remodelling of this splendid edifice. To be viewed the day prior to the sale, and catalogues had at the auctioneer's offices, 28, Chancery-lane. – The Times, 12 October 1842.

The pulpit was advertised in four sales, before it found a buyer. The catalogue for the final sale emphasised ominously that the lots – 'the magnificent carved DOORS, pillasters, and screens, from the Temple Church, 60 feet long...' – would be sold without reserve; so unfashionable had such classical woodwork become.

The organ was moved to its present position in the 1840s, when the Round and Chancel were reunited. In 1909-10 the organ would be rebuilt by Frederick Rothwell; his tonal extensions and impovements were clearly a triumph. Rothwell installed (his own patented invention) ivory tabs above each manual to replace the traditional draw-stops on either side of the console.

To mark the opening of the refurbished Church, the Inns retained a small choir of men and boys. In 1843 they appointed E.J. Hopkins as Organist, confirmed the establishment of the choir and reordered the stalls to give the music a greater prominence. The choir has ever since been one of the most celebrated church choirs in London. Hopkins, the founder of Anglican psalmody, was in post for 55 years. He was succeeded by Henry Walford Davies, who encouraged the Inns to take on as his assistant the young George Thalben-Ball. Sir George was at the Temple from 1919 until 1981. In 1927, under Thalben-Ball, the Temple chorister Ernest Lough recorded Mendelssohn's 'O, for the Wings of a Dove' in the Church. It is as famous as any recording ever made: it has been available ever since 1927; more than five million copies have been sold.

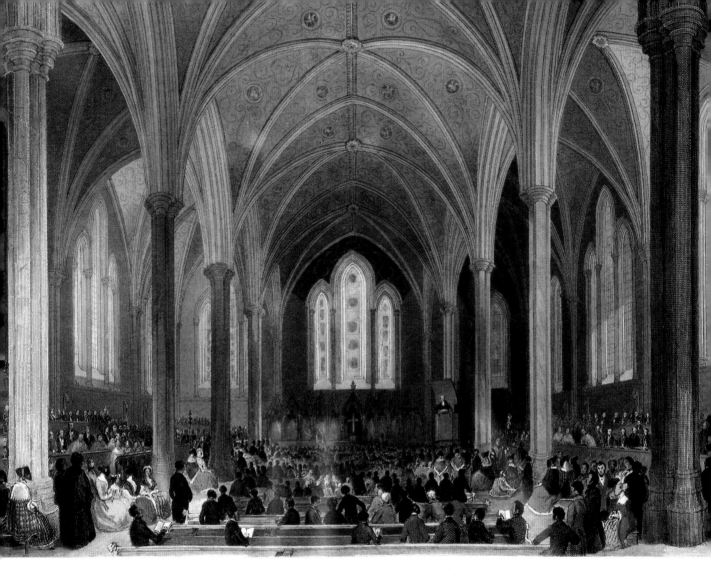

G. Cattermole and H. Melville, 1843: The Chancel.

64

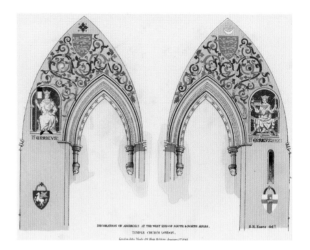

Designs by T. Willement for the windows and by R.H. Essex for the painted decoration of the Church, 1843.

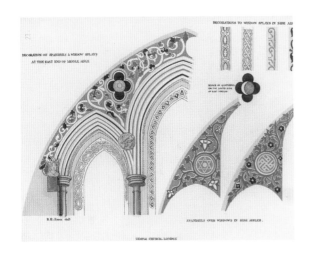

Upper Compartment.

By 1048 the Church of the Holy Sepulchre in Jerusalem had a steep conical roof; the Crusaders captured Jerusalem in 1099, and that steep cone became, throughout the medieval West, the most famous feature of the complex. The photograph on the right shows the Round's roof built in emulation, in the 1860s. On the right is Lamb Building, destroyed in World War II.

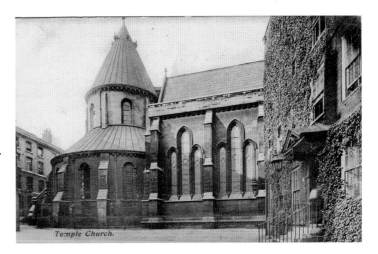

Temple Church.

H. Woodward (silversmith), 1880: Dessert Service, made for Middle Temple, the plateau 1625mm long. The plateau bears two emblems: the Templars' symbol of two knights on one horse; and the arms of the Treasurer of Middle Temple in 1880. The large epergnes are each supported by three knights standing fully armed. Their shields bear different devices: one, the lion rampant of the Marshals, Earls of Pembroke (three of whom are buried in the Church, with effigies); one, the arms then attributed to Geoffrey de Mandeville (also buried in the Church, with an effigy); one, the arms of Middle Temple.

The refurbishment of the sanctuary by S. Smirke and D. Burton, 1843, was clearly not regarded as a success. In 1908 Reginald Blomfield redesigned the area, as above. In 1929 this altarpiece was removed in its turn, and replaced by a simple curtain; by the time of World War II this as well had been removed and the aumbries revealed (see p. 25).

10 MAY 1941

The night of 10 May 1941 was fine and moonlit. The river was at low ebb; water pressure was weak. The sirens sounded at 11.00pm; the raid lasted all night. By morning, five Livery Company Halls had been destroyed; the Mint, Mansion House, Tower and British Museum had all been damaged; the House of Commons Chamber had been burnt out, Westminster Hall and the Abbey scarred.

An early bomb landed in Middle Temple Gardens and destroyed the water mains. Around midnight fire-watchers saw an incendiary land on the roof of the Church, at the south-east angle of the chancel. The fire caught hold on the chancel roof; it spread to the vestries, to the organ and so down to the wooden furnishings inside the Church itself. The heat split the Chancel's columns, but the vault held up; the wooden roof of the Round caved in on the knights' effigies below.

The fire was still burning in the Round at noon on the next day. In the Chancel the pews and choir-stalls had been reduced to lines of ash. The Smith-Rothwell organ was destroyed beyond recognition. In the Church's lobby, at the south door, is a painting by Kathleen Allen (1906-1983) of one effigy as it appeared on 11 May.

The fire spread to Lamb Building (in the centre of the present Church Court) and burnt it out. 'At two o'clock in the morning,' wrote the Senior Warden, 'it was as light as day. Charred papers and embers were flying through the air, bombs and shrapnel all around. It was an awe-inspiring sight.' On the same night Inner Temple's Hall, Parliament Chamber and Library, the Cloisters and large parts of Pump Court were destroyed.

It was seventeen years before the Church itself was fully repaired. The cracked columns were all replaced, with new stone from the beds of Purbeck 'marble' quarried in the Middle Ages. The Chancel's columns had been famous for tilting outwards; they were rebuilt at the same angle. The tomb of the learned and courageous John Selden – who stood out against the abuse of executive power in the 17th century – was rediscovered under the south-west corner of the Chancel. The East Window, a gift from the Worshipful Company of Glaziers, was designed and built by Carl Edwards; the central window and a key to its scenes are shown overleaf.

The Round Church under Repair, in The Illustrated London News, 1947.
Collection: Guildhall Library, City of London

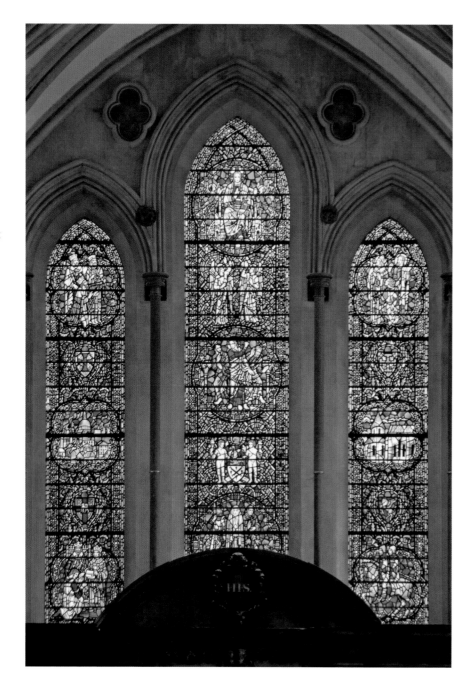

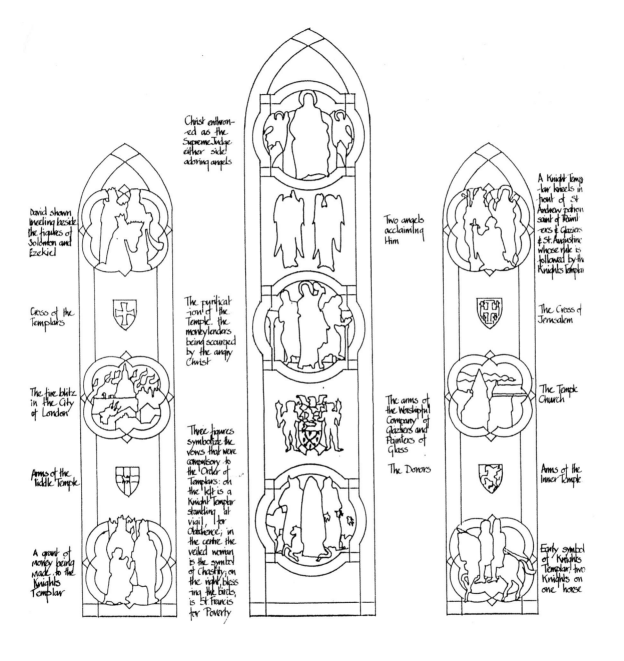

David shown kneeling beside the figures of Solomon and Ezekiel

Cross of the Templars

The fire blitz in the City of London

Arms of the Middle Temple

A grant of money being made to the Knights Templar

Christ enthroned as the Supreme Judge either side adoring angels

The purification of the Temple, the moneylenders being scourged by the angry Christ

Three figures symbolize the vows that were compulsory to the Order of Templars: on the left is a Knight Templar standing at vigil, for Obedience; in the centre the veiled woman is the symbol of Chastity; on the right, blessing the birds, is St Francis for Poverty

Two angels acclaiming Him

The arms of the Worshipful Company of Glaziers and Painters of Glass

The Donors

A Knight Templar kneels in front of St Andrew patron saint of Painters & Glaziers & St Augustine whose rule is followed by the Knights Templar

The Cross of Jerusalem

The Temple Church

Arms of the Inner Temple

Early symbol of Knights Templar, two Knights on one horse

Facing page: The rededication of the Round Church on 7 November 1958 by the Archbishop of Canterbury in the presence of The Queen, Prince Philip and Queen Elizabeth The Queen Mother. The Chancel had already been rededicated in the presence of Queen Elizabeth The Queen Mother on 23 March 1954. Her Majesty The Queen revisited the Church and inspected the Letters Patent on 26 June 1985, to celebrate the 800th Anniversary of the consecration of the Round Church.

The Temple Church is a beautiful building: a perfect setting for our full programme of concerts and lectures, and a welcome oasis of peace and quiet within yards of Fleet Street. Here we can stand back from the City's busy-ness and rediscover our place within 800 years of history.

In the Church we remember as well a longer history still: of God's loving purpose for all creation, wholly revealed in the person, life, work, death and rising of Jesus. It is both humbling and inspiring to be the heirs of Richard Hooker, Master of the Temple at a time – in the 1580s – of great national danger and division. Hooker wrote of the Eucharist, the focus in his day of intense debate:

> Christ assisting this heavenly banquet with his personal and true presence doth by his own divine power add to the natural substance thereof supernatural efficacy, which addition to the nature of those consecrated elements changeth them and maketh them that unto us which otherwise they could not be... To us they are thereby made such instruments as mystically yet truly, invisibly yet really work both our communion or fellowship with the person of Jesus Christ, as well in that he is man as God; and our participation also in the fruit, grace and efficacy of his body and blood...Hereupon there ensueth a kind of transubstantiation in us, a true change both of soul and body, an alteration from death to life.

We pray, live and work for such a transubstantiation in ourselves and in all who come to this special place. We hope you will have an opportunity to return.

THE CHARTER WINDOW, 2008

Illustrated on the back cover is the Charter Window commissioned by Inner and Middle Temple to mark the Quatercentenary of the Letters Patent (1608). The window, designed and built by Caroline Benyon, is in the central bay of the Church's south side. On the left- and right- hand lights are the symbols of the two Inns: the Pegasus of Inner Temple, and the Lamb and Flag of Middle. In the centre light, the scales of justice are suspended from the centrally positioned sword. Either side of the crown are symbols from the Coat of Arms of King James VI of Scotland and I of England: the three lions guardant of England and Scottish lion rampant; the Irish harp and the fleur d'lys of France are below. Beati pacifici, 'Blessed are the Peacemakers,' was the King's motto. The Commonwealth symbol and the stars of the EU are incorporated near the base of the design.

Caroline Benyon's father, Carl Edwards, designed the Church's East Window.

＊＊

The standard work on the Church's architecture, monuments and decoration is now R. Griffith-Jones and D. Park (editors), The Temple Church (Woodbridge: Boydell, 2010). Robin Griffith-Jones compiled this book with debts on every page, in particular to E. Richardson, Monumental Effigies of the Temple Church…(London: Longman, 1843) and The Ancient Stone and Leaden Coffins etc…lately discovered in the Temple Church (London: Longman, 1845); Mrs A. Esdaile, Temple Church Monuments (London: Barber, 1933); J.B. Williamson, The History of the Temple, London (London: John Murray, 1924); B.A. Lees, Records of the Templars in England in the Twelfth Century (London: British Academy, 1935); W.H. Godfrey, 'Recent Discoveries at the Temple, London….', Archaeologia 95 (1953), 123-40; D. Lewer and R. Dark, The Temple Church in London (London: Historical Publications, 1997); J. Butler, Saxons, Templars and Lawyers in the Inner Temple (London: PCA Monograph Series 4, 2005). All errors are the responsibility of the compiler. In case you have been drawn to the Church by The Da Vinci Code, you may like to see R. Griffith-Jones, The Da Vinci Code and the Secrets of the Temple (London: SCM-Canterbury and Grand Rapids: Eerdmans, 2006).

We gratefully acknowledge permission to reproduce photographs as follows: The Society of Antiquaries of London (19, 28); The Ashmolean Museum, Oxford (6-7); The Bowes Museum, Barnard Castle (48; bottom); The Burrell Collection, Glasgow (21; top); Guildhall Library, City of London (46 and 47, 49, 56, 57; top, 74; top, 75); The Dean and Chapter of Hereford Cathedral and the Hereford Mappa Mundi Trust (11); The Museum of London (21; bottom, 26; bottom, 37); Nina Large (80; mid-right and bottom-left); Chris Christodoulou (front and back covers, 9, 17, 19, 20, 24, 25; bottom, 26; top, 27, 29, 35, 38, 41, 50, 51, 52, 54, 59, 63, 76, 82 and 83); Rod Natkiel (80; mid-left); Miranda Parry of MPP Image Creation (79; bottom-right, 80; top-left); Reginald Piggott (12, 14, 22); Kenneth Richardson (5); Philippe Terrancle (2); Simon Tottman (80; bottom-right). Other photos are provided by courtesy of Inner or Middle Temple.